ALLEN PHOTO

THE GOLDEN RETRIEVER

CONTENTS

BREED CHARACTERISTICS

The gentle, fun-loving nature, together with the endless willingness to please are undoubtedly the most endearing characteristics of the Golden Retriever. They thrive on the day-to-day family life and their nature makes them one of the most suitable pets, being very much a 'peoples' dog. They are not so active that they drive you mad but are as active as you want them to be. A Golden can be lying down, apparently asleep, but if you so much as pick up their lead they come to life immediately, tail wagging and ready to go.

Ready for a walk *KIPPS*

Different head types and colouring within the breed *KIPPS*

Colour can vary enormously and can be any shade from pale cream to rich gold but not red. The coat's texture can also vary considerably. It can be either straight or wavy and some also have more length to their feathering than others but both are correct. They should carry a full dentition with a scissor bite, i.e. the top teeth closely covering the bottom ones.

Two top winning show dogs of different type and colouring. Both are correct and fit within the breed standard

Correct scissor bite *KIPPS*

Their appearance is of a balanced symmetrical shape and should be constructed totally in proportion. They have a kind, gentle head and a soft, appealing expression and a dense water-resistant coat with ample featherings on tail, trousers, tummy and front legs. If left untrimmed a Golden will have quite a 'ruff' under his head down his front and if he is a show dog then this 'ruff' is trimmed to show off the neck and shoulder assembly, giving a clean outline.

An untrimmed neck showing the natural 'ruff' *KIPPS*

A trimmed neck, enhancing the clean shoulder line *KIPPS*

They should have round, cat-like feet with thick pads, straight front legs set well under the body. The rear has a

Round 'cat-like' feet *KIPPS*

Balanced, symmetrical shape *KIPPS*

Black nose *KIPPS*

Brown/pink nose *KIPPS*

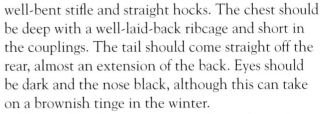

well-bent stifle and straight hocks. The chest should be deep with a well-laid-back ribcage and short in the couplings. The tail should come straight off the rear, almost an extension of the back. Eyes should be dark and the nose black, although this can take on a brownish tinge in the winter.

The Golden Retriever is a gundog and therefore should look as though he could do a day's work in the field, i.e. an athletic body without surplus fat which can 'roll' as he moves. A fit dog is a healthy dog! He should move freely, with long, flowing strides, covering the ground with ease and apparently no effort at all. Goldens are proud dogs and tend to love to show off when moving, holding their head in such a manner as if to say 'look at me – I'm the greatest'. They love to be admired and made a fuss of by everyone they come in contact with.

There are many varying 'types' of Goldens and this is usually determined by the different breeding lines that are put together and whether the matings

A good example of a healthy dog *KIPPS*

Goldens love to work and make ideal working gundogs *KIPPS*

are 'line bred' on certain lines (common ancestors) or 'outcrossed' (different ancestors), but all types are correct and should possess the same characteristics and the typical 'Golden' temperament. A bad-tempered or aggressive Golden is relatively rare and most certainly not the norm.

Goldens should not portray fear and should have a confident nature being able to cope with most situations. They put utmost trust in their owners, trusting them implicitly.

Being gundogs, they usually have a natural, inbuilt hunting ability, hence when out for exercise they will almost certainly spend a great deal of time with their nose to the ground.

CHOICE AND CARE OF THE PUPPY

Having decided that a Golden Retriever is the breed you would like, how do you select a puppy?

One of the best ways to go about this is to contact the Kennel Club and obtain a list of the breed clubs, of which there are many in different regions of the country. The breed club secretary will have a list of reputable breeders in your area. To be able to register a litter with the club, the breeder is asked to supply relevant details about the puppies, i.e. if the parents have eye certificates and their hips have been X-rayed and scored to ensure they are sound. It is essential to purchase from a reputable breeder, who has done everything in their power to breed a litter which will be as sound and healthy as possible and with the correct 'Golden' temperament.

Which one? They all look appealing *KIPPS*

Once you have found a 'suitable' litter you will be asked numerous questions by the breeder, who has to ensure that you will make responsible owners and will look after the puppy to the very best of your ability – making sure that you realise what a great commitment you are taking on. From your point of view, always ask to see the dam of the puppies and if possible the sire also. The litter should be strong, healthy and outgoing.

Having made your choice, the breeder will give you as much help and advice as you require. Check that the puppy has under-

This puppy receives his first injection

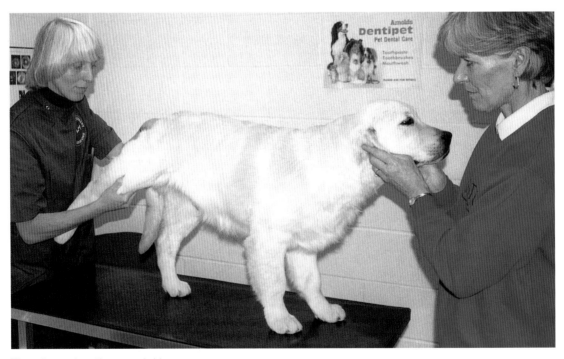

The vet examines the puppy's hips

Early lead training *KIPPS*

gone a worming programme and ask for feeding instructions. It is always best to continue feeding the same food, to avoid upsetting the puppy's tummy – it is a big enough ordeal for the puppy to undertake going to a new environment without having to adjust to a change of diet as well.

Check with your vet when the puppy is due to have his first injection; until the puppy has completed the first course of injections he cannot enter into the outside world, as he could very easily contact disease. At the first visit the vet will give the puppy a thorough examination to ensure all is well. One week after the second (or last) injection you are then able to take the puppy out of his confined environment. During this restricted time, you can get the puppy used to a collar and lead in the garden, so that when the time comes to venture out he is quite comfortable walking on the lead. It is also helpful to take the puppy on short, frequent car journeys so that he gets used to the motion of the car. Most dogs grow to travel extremely well in the car and associate it with a good experience.

Becoming accustomed to the car *KIPPS*

House training should be started immediately the puppy arrives home and generally they catch on quickly. Always put the puppy outside after a meal, on waking and at frequent intervals during the day. If he starts walking round in circles, sniffing the ground, then he needs to go out. When he has 'performed' praise him so that he knows he has done the right thing. Goldens generally become clean quickly and they very rarely soil their beds, preferring to do their business in a designated area. They are an intelligent breed and learn very quickly.

Once the puppy is able to go out it is most important to get him used to as many different things and experiences as possible, so that he can cope with almost any situation he comes across. The puppy will then grow up to become well-adjusted and sociably acceptable. Most towns have dog societies which run training classes, either obedience or ringcraft (for training show dogs), a few visits to these classes is of invaluable experience for the young dog, it teaches them how to behave in the presence of other dogs and gets them used to obeying commands in the presence of distractions (i.e. other dogs). Goldens are usually easy to train as they have such a will to please and do not like doing wrong. It is extremely important to teach a puppy right from wrong in the home from the outset. Much like young children, they have to learn what they can and cannot do. If the puppy is doing something he should not be doing, then a sharp 'no' suffices and distracts his attention. Your tone of voice is usually sufficient to reprimand the puppy, they do not like it when you are displeased and they can tell by your voice. Always remember to praise him when he is good.

A reward for being good *KIPPS*

FEEDING

When you bring your new puppy home, you should be given a diet sheet from the breeder. This will state exactly how much, when and what your puppy is fed. Usually at eight weeks the puppy is still on four meals a day – breakfast, lunch, tea and supper. Gradually as the puppy grows and gets older the four meals will be reduced to three, then two and as an adult he can be fed either once or twice a day, whichever suits you.

This seventeen-week old puppy is the correct weight for his age *KIPPS*

The first meal to cut out should be the last meal of the day. This will enable him to go through the night without needing to relieve himself and consequently he will be clean at night sooner. The puppy usually tells you himself when he needs the number of feeds to be reduced, as he will start 'picking' at his food and not completely finishing each meal.

When feeding your puppy, give him five to ten minutes to eat his fill and if any food is left, remove it and make him wait until the next meal time. If he is allowed to nibble all day he will never be hungry enough to eat a full meal and could also put on too much weight. I usually have my puppies on two meals by six months of age and then by twelve months down to one meal a day – as I prefer to feed my adult dogs once a day as opposed to twice. It is what suits me and is personal preference.

Different breeders have different preferences and ideas about what to feed their puppies and dogs. Usually if you find a food you are happy with you tend to stick with the food and do not constantly keep changing and trying different foods, this can also upset the stomach of the puppy or

Puppy and adult dog enjoying a feed *KIPPS*

dog. I prefer to feed a complete dried food, which I know is properly balanced and needs no additives whatsoever. It is important not to oversupplement a growing puppy, as too much can be just as harmful as not enough. Most of the manufacturers do a complete range of diets, starting from puppy, going on to junior, then to adult and lastly one for the not so active or older dog. You can also get a high protein food for very active or working dogs and a sensitive one for dogs with digestive problems. The complete ranges are readily available from supermarkets, pet shops and also some veterinary practices.

Some people prefer to feed a more 'natural' diet with fresh meat, vegetables etc. but the preparation for this is more time consuming and you need to be very sure and knowledgeable about the nutrients included, ensuring that there are sufficient and that not too many vitamin supplements are added.

If at any time your dog has an upset tummy, resulting in diarrhoea and/or sickness, it is always advisable to starve him completely for about twenty-four hours and then gradually give him rice, eggs and chicken until he is back to normal. Do not try to overload his stomach to make up for lost time. Take it slowly and usually within a few days he will be back to normal and if not, seek veterinary advice.

Different types of feed for different needs *KIPPS*

A fit and healthy adult dog enjoying his exercise *KIPPS*

Always ensure that you monitor carefully your dog's intake of food, just give the odd titbit as a reward and not every time you see him or from the meal table, as a fat dog is not a healthy dog. It is especially important not to have your puppy too heavy whilst he is growing as it puts undue strain on his joints and he could have problems later in life, especially with his hips. So be patient, wait until your dog matures naturally, do not try to force him to look 'a big boy' by overfeeding. He will be a far healthier dog if he is carrying the correct weight, and will be fitter and live a long, active life.

If you wish to feed your dog or puppy a bone, never feed any type that can 'splinter', the most suitable ones are cooked knuckle bones.

The aim of correct feeding is to have a fit and healthy dog with strong bones and teeth.

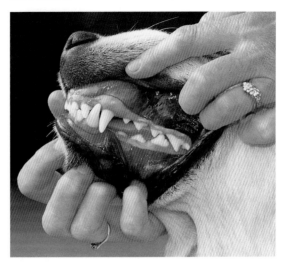

Teeth and gums should be strong, clean and healthy *KIPPS*

GROOMING

Grooming is an essential part of the day-to-day care of your dog. A long coat needs regular attention to maintain its condition. Nothing looks worse than a Golden with a matted look to their coat. Daily grooming of ten minutes or so is all that is needed to keep your dog looking as though 'somebody owns him'. It is best to start as soon as the new puppy has settled in, a daily comb or brush at this early stage and he will be used to it for the rest of his life. They usually love the fuss and attention and I always find my dogs queue

Puppy getting used to a daily brush *KIPPS*

up to be groomed. With a small puppy, it is best to use a soft brush and a comb but when he starts to change his coat and gets his adult coat, a stronger 'slicker' type brush is better to get through the length and density of his coat. Use a comb for the featherings.

Grooming equipment, available from most pet shops *KIPPS*

An adult dog having a daily groom *KIPPS*

Always ensure that the dog's nails are kept neat and relatively short. If he is walked regularly on concrete or a hard surface (i.e. pavement), the nails should wear down naturally and not need clipping but if your dog is exercised mostly on soft ground (i.e. grass), he may occasionally need the ends of his nails taken off with nail clippers. Always be careful not to clip them too short; if the pink quick of the nail is cut (the soft part in the middle of the nail) it will bleed, temporarily.

Nail clipping *KIPPS*

Goldens do lose their hair – males usually once a year and females twice to coincide with their seasons. When they start to lose their hair, it is always best to step up the daily, regular grooming and try to get the dead hair out as quickly as possible. Apart from the loose hairs being a total nuisance, if they are removed the new coat is encouraged to grow more quickly. You can usually tell when the coat is about to come out, as the texture changes, becoming dry, almost brittle and losing its shine. You can buy special combs from the pet shop to assist in the removal of the dead hair and to de-tangle any knots that may appear in the coat.

above An 'out of coat' Golden *below* 'In coat' Golden KIPPS

Always ensure that your dog's ears are cleaned on a regular basis. Ear cleansing lotions are easily obtainable from most pet stores or from the vet. Keeping them clean will help to avoid any ear infections. Teeth are usually easy to keep clean if bones or chewable toys are given but if you notice that this is insufficient, then you can clean them as you would your own. It is important to keep the teeth clean as this reduces the likelihood of infected gums.

It is most important to keep the ear canal clean KIPPS

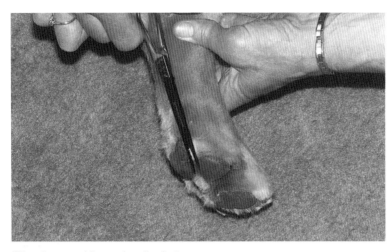

Trimming round the pad on the feet *KIPPS*

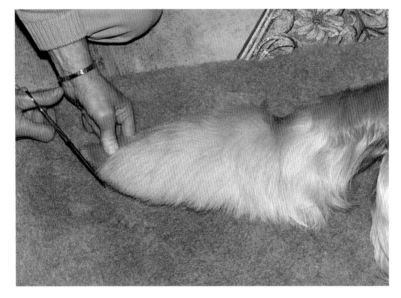

Keep the feet of your dog trimmed and this will help to avoid excess dirt and mud being brought into the house as well as giving a well-shaped foot. With a pair of straight-edged scissors trim around the edges of each pad. The tail also looks neater trimmed. Do this by starting at the end of the tail and trim to form a neat curve, getting longer towards the base of the tail.

If the eyes look at all sore or red, firstly clean them with warm, boiled water and cotton wool, if no improvement in a couple of days, seek veterinary advice.

Daily, regular grooming enables you to check over your dog to ensure that all is well and also they really do love the fuss!

A 'trimmed' tail looks neater *KIPPS*

BASIC TRAINING

It is essential and most important to train your dog so that he is a sociably acceptable part of the family. There is nothing worse than having a totally unruly dog in the house and it is most embarrassing for all concerned when anyone comes to visit. If you have a dog that you can control, you can feel proud when visited and not feel that you have to constantly apologise for his behaviour.

Basic training should start as soon as you bring your puppy home and it is imperative that he learns the fundamentals of what he can and what he cannot do. Be precise and positive in your corrections, the best way at an early age is to distract him from what he is doing wrong and transfer his attention onto something else. Goldens are quick to learn and do not like to be chastised.

Lead training can commence in the confines of your own garden, during the time he is unable to go out prior to completing his course of first injections. Put an appropriate puppy collar on him for short periods so that he gets used to having something around his neck. He will probably sit and scratch at first but will soon become accustomed to this 'foreign body' around him. Next clip the lead onto the collar and get him used to being led, so that when the time comes for him to enter the big wide world outside, he has become quite used to walking with a lead and collar. There are more than enough new experiences for him to cope with so one less does ease the situation for him.

A puppy, now accustomed to walking on a lead, strides out *KIPPS*

Get him out and about as much as possible in the early days so that he can gain as many new experiences as possible. Do not, however, take him on long marathon walks but on short, frequent ones.

Puppies are inquisitive so be on your guard! *KIPPS*

Once he has become accustomed to the surroundings outside, you can then start his lead training and basic obedience without so many distractions.

This early training is of the utmost importance so that you can both enjoy the many years ahead.

Having gained your dog's trust and when you are quite happy that he responds to you, it is then time to let him off the lead. At the onset of this exercise it is useful to carry a few titbits in your pocket and to keep calling him back to you, giving him a reward for doing as he is told. If this sounds like bribery, it is, but it works! In a relatively short period of time he will learn to respond to your basic commands. Always use the same command for the same instruction to avoid confusing him with what is expected of him.

Always remember that you are the one taking the dog for a walk and not the other way round!

Young dogs experiencing their first outing to the beach *KIPPS*

Start your training with a soft puppy collar and lead, then progress to a stronger collar and lead or either a rope or leather slip lead. Very, very seldom would I recommend, or indeed would you need to use, a choke chain to restrict and train your Golden.

Selection of types of lead *KIPPS*

Do practise frequently, making him sit and stay, as this is an invaluable exercise to ensure he is sociably well behaved when you take him to public places, where invariably there are other dogs and people. People can get quite upset if they are out for a stroll, dressed in their Sunday best, when a wet, dirty dog comes bounding along and jumps up to say 'hello' – I wonder why?

Basic retrieving training can begin when your Golden is a puppy but for dogs under twelve months, the retrieving sessions must be kept short.

Teaching 'sit and stay' KIPPS

Adult dog accustomed to 'sit and stay' KIPPS

Do make it fun – he should love it. As he gets older, more advance commands and training can be introduced. The older dog has a longer concentration span than a young one.

right A puppy learning to retrieve a dummy, a task they love to learn
KIPPS

A more experienced adult dog retrieving

Golden Retrievers can also be trained to do tricks!

FIRST AID

It is always sound advice to do a daily check of ears, eyes and feet whilst grooming to check for any abnormalities. This practice also gets the dog used to being handled so that when a vet needs to examine him he is used to it.

I will mention a few of the more common things that may be useful to have knowledge of so that you feel able to cope if confronted with the situation.

ROAD TRAFFIC ACCIDENT

Your dog may appear normal after a road accident. It is often difficult to assess the dog's injuries but there could be internal haemorrhaging, a vital organ could be damaged or ribs broken.

Keep calm, speak gently to the dog and let him see you approach, put pressure on any open, visible wounds, keep him as quiet and warm as possible and get to the veterinary surgery as quickly as possible. If necessary use a muzzle. Do not leave him as he will need professional treatment. He could be suffering from shock, signs of which are lack of colour in the gums and below the lower eyelids, distressed, rapid and shallow breathing, weak, rapid or irregular pulse, glassy-eyed appearance, cold and shivering with a clammy skin, rapid and shallow breathing.

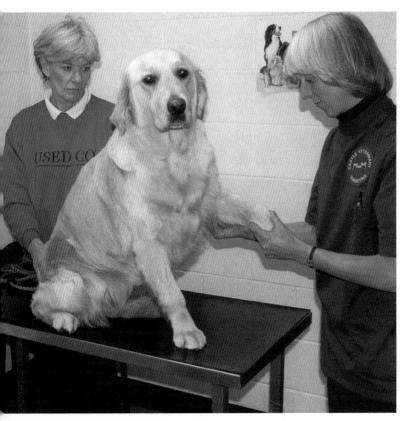

Checking for lameness in the front legs

FRACTURES

Keep the injured limb as still as possible, do not attempt to handle the limb to splint it. If the skin is broken try to protect the wound from contamination by covering it with a clean piece of cloth. If there is a lot of bleeding try to apply pressure to the wound until veterinary advice is sought. He will undoubtedly need to have an X-ray to determine the extent of the injury.

LAMENESS

There can be many causes of lameness in dogs, from a simple strain to more serious conditions. It is always advisable to check the pads first to eliminate a cut or foreign body embedded in the pad. If there is no obvious reason why he has gone lame, try resting him for a few days to see if he becomes sound, if there is no sign of improvement then take him to the vet, who will carry out more extensive examinations. There can be many reasons why dogs go lame and some conditions can only be diagnosed by X-raying the offending part.

INSECT STINGS

Stings do not usually cause serious problems and normally appear on the face or lips. If the 'sting' is visible, try to remove it with a pair of tweezers. The sting will cause a localised swelling, some irritation and pain but generally is a relatively short-lived problem. Cold, damp cloths can be applied to the swelling area if on the face. However, if the sting goes into the blood stream or the dog is allergic to it, do not hesitate to seek veterinary advice.

ECZEMA

There are two different types of eczema: wet and dry. Whatever the cause, the dog starts to nibble, lick and scratch, this results in a patch of eczema. Most cases are treatable by simple remedies, part the hair from the affected area and cleanse with a non-toxic disinfectant. If it is no better after a couple of days or so then the vet will probably need to prescribe some medication to be taken to help speed up the healing process.

WORMS

Regular worming of your dog is essential for the well-being of his health and condition. Three to four times a year is recommended with an appropriate preparation from your vet. It is also most important for the health of any small children who may come in contact with the dog and it must be emphasised that you must not leave your dog's faeces in public places – it is your responsibility to clean up after your dog.

FLEAS

At the first sign of your dog scratching or routinely twice a year, treat your dog for fleas. Use one of the appropriate preparations on the market, of which there are

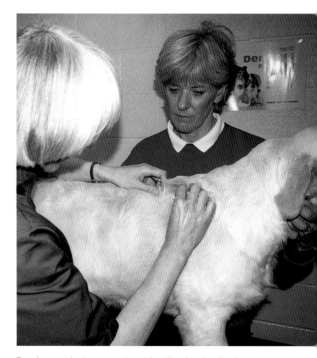

Dog's coat being examined for 'foreign bodies'

sprays, powder and also a liquid which is put on the skin on the back of the neck and is effective for up to four weeks. If in any doubt about which to use, your vet will recommend which type is preferable for your dog.

VACCINATIONS

It is recommended by veterinary surgeons that a yearly booster is given, after the initial course of injections as a puppy. The injections are a preventative against certain diseases which can be picked up by your dog in the day-to-day exercising routine or, in fact, by being in contact with affected animals, for example: distemper, hepatitis, canine parvovirus, para influenza and leptospirosis. Vaccinations are not expensive compared to the cost should your dog contract one of these diseases which could even be fatal and you cannot put a price on peace of mind.

EAR INFECTIONS

These can usually be avoided by regular cleaning of the ears using appropriate cleansing solutions. If there is any foul smell or discharge coming from the ear canal do not hesitate to seek veterinary advice.

A puppy having an examination of the ear canal

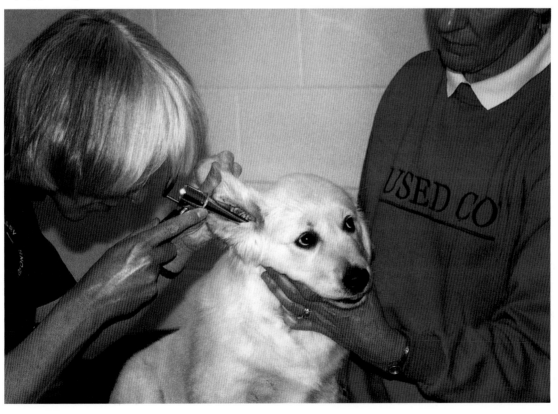

EYES

If for any reason the eye(s) start weeping or discharging, bathe with warm, boiled water and if there is no improvement in a couple of days seek expert advice. You cannot afford to take any chances with the delicate structure of the eyes.

BLOAT

With this condition the animal's abdomen starts to swell and feels like a tight drum, breathing becomes laboured and the dog will show discomfort in a short space of time; it can be fatal if veterinary help is not sought immediately. To help prevent this condition, do not feed one hour before or one hour after exercise.

Eye examination

CUT PAD

Clean the wound, apply pressure and bandage if possible. If the cut looks very deep it may need stitching. Clean with salt water or a weak disinfectant solution. If any foreign body is visible, try to remove it and if this is not possible keep it clean and dry until veterinary advice is sought.

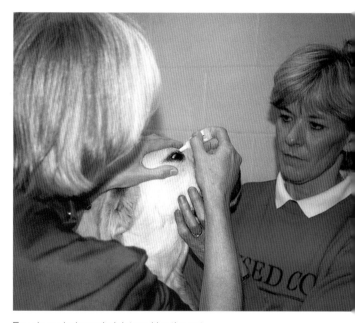

Eye drops being administered by the vet

POISONS

If the poisoning is the result of a tablet overdose (i.e. not corrosive), make the animal sick immediately. To do this give the dog soda crystals or mustard and water. Corrosive poison needs advice from the vet who will want to know how much was taken, what it was and if possible to see the packet. Wash off poisons from the animal's coat, if it is an oily material use Swarfega to rub into the coat and then wash with mild detergent.

BURNS AND SCALDS

If relevant wipe off any hot cooking oil, grease etc., do not clip hair or apply creams/ointments. Douse the wound with cold water, if possible cover the area with a cold compress. Take at once to the veterinary surgeon.

HEAT STROKE

This typically occurs when a dog is in a confined space during hot weather. The dog will show signs of distress and will be panting hard for air. The body temperature must be reduced at once by dousing in cold water, then cover with a wet sheet and contact the veterinary surgeon, even if the dog appears normal.

It is important to establish a good relationship with your veterinary practice

A good relationship should be established with your veterinary surgeon, as you put your complete trust in their knowledge and I advise you to take out insurance cover for your dog as prolonged veterinary treatment can become expensive.

USEFUL ADDRESSES

For details of breed clubs contact:
The Kennel Club
1 Clarges Street,
London W1Y 8AB

In America contact:
The American Kennel Club
4th Floor,
260 Madison Avenue,
New York NY 10016/2401

In Germany contact:
Verband fur das Deutsche Hundewesen (VDH)
Westfalendamm 174,
44141 Dortmund,
Germany

ACKNOWLEDGEMENTS

I am most grateful to Castle Veterinary Surgeons, Barnard Castle,
for all their help and support especially with the First Aid section.
I am also grateful to them for help with photographs.
My grateful thanks also go to Lynn Kipps who undertook the majority
of the photographic work for this book.

Dedication

To my husband Dave, for his unfailing support

British Library Cataloguing-in-Publication Data.
A catalogue record for this book is available from the British Library

ISBN 0.85131.775.8

Published in Great Britain in 2000 by
J. A. Allen an imprint of Robert Hale Ltd.,
Clerkenwell House, 45–47 Clerkenwell Green,
London EC1R 0HT

Series design by Paul Saunders, layout by Dick Vine
Series editor John Beaton
Colour processing by Tenon & Polert Colour Scanning Ltd., Hong Kong
Printed in Hong Kong by Dah Hua International Printing Press Co. Ltd.